Quick
Answers to
Tough
Questions

CREATION

EVOLUTION

BIBLE

Information

40%   46%   15%

BRYAN OSBORNE
& BODIE HODGE

First printing: July 2017
Fourth printing: August 2019

ISBN: 978-1-68344-010-9
ISBN: 978-1-61458-607-4 (digital)
Library of Congress Number: 2017907703

Cover by Diana Bogardus

Unless otherwise noted, Scripture quotations are from the New King James Version of the Bible.

Please consider requesting that a copy of this volume be purchased by your local library system.

Printed in China

Please visit our website for other great titles:
www.masterbooks.com

Master
Books®
A Division of New Leaf Publishing Group
www.masterbooks.com

For information regarding author interviews,
please contact the publicity department at (870) 438-5288.

Photo and Illustration Credits:

Unless otherwise noted, all images are from shutterstock.com

Ark Encounter/Creation Museum: p. 13, 47, 51, 61, 77

Bryan Osborne: p. 47

Bill Looney: p 75

Wikimedia Commons: Images from Wikimedia Commons are used under the CC0 1.0, CC BY-SA 2.0 DE,
CC-BY-SA-3.0 license or the GNU Free Documentation License, Version 1.3.
p. 41, 43, 57, 69

Foreword

In this electronic age, I'm often checking my smartphone for emails, posting items to Facebook, and taking care of other tasks using our wonderful modern-day technology. So, I'm finding it increasingly difficult to keep up my habit of reading books, magazines, and other literature that are printed on good-old-fashioned paper.

Quick Answers to Tough Questions is a perfect resource for those of us who can get so absorbed with electronic media reading a printed book becomes a challenge. So for brevity sake, the authors have provided readers with a series of mini articles on a variety of topics.

This book is ideal for teens and adults looking for brief Bible-upholding and science-confirming answers to some of the most-asked questions of our day. Take a peek, for example, at page 38. Right there, in less than 400 words, Bryan and Bodie give an excellent answer to the question "Why is there death and suffering if there is a God?" That's a question that many non-Christians (and even many Christians) struggle with today.

Quick Answers to Tough Questions is your handy tool that offers relevant answers to many of the pressing questions people have. It is dedicated to upholding the authority of God's Word, from its very first verse, and to answering the skeptics of our day. Of course, the gospel is presented in the book.

Today, it's unfortunate to see so many pastors and other church leaders not taking a stand on God's Word, starting in Genesis. Should we be surprised, then, that the church is not affecting the culture as it once did in our Christianized countries? Indeed, our Western nations are becoming more secular every year.

Over the decades, I have been deeply saddened to see a huge exodus of young people from our churches. The "seeker-sensitive" approach, prominent in so many churches nowadays (often with an emphasis on entertainment), has overtaken the teaching of God's Word as the top priority. As a result, generations do not know what they believe, much less why they believe it. More than ever, our young people and adults need to be equipped with answers to defend the Christian faith against the secular attacks of the day—confident in knowing they can trust God's Word from Genesis to Revelation.

As Answers in Genesis seeks to help usher in a new reformation within our churches so that once again they will impact the culture for the gospel, it's thrilling that apologists like Bryan and Bodie are leading the charge. They are producing excellent resources like this book that defend the Christian faith and proclaim the gospel.

Yes, the spiritual struggle is an enormous one—and at times the battle can be daunting. But by becoming better-equipped, Christians can be more effective in engaging the culture for Christ.

Thanks for putting down your smartphone or other electronic device to read this book. I know you'll be blessed by Bryan and Bodie's wonderful apologetics resource.

~ Ken Ham,
president/CEO of Answers in Genesis

Introduction

What is going on in our culture?

What is happening? To the honest observer, it is clear that America is undergoing a rapid moral and cultural revolution of unprecedented momentum. America is becoming less Christian and more secular with each passing moment. We now live in a culture where the Bible, prayer, Christian symbols, and Christianity as a whole are increasingly attacked and marginalized. And it's all taking place in a nation founded on many biblical principles!

This revolution is not limited to America; it's happening all across the Western World. But the fact it is happening in America is quite astonishing. Why? Because America is one of the most "Christianized" nations ever. Right now it has more Christian resources (churches, seminaries, Christian colleges, bookstores, TV and radio stations, etc.) than any other nation has ever had throughout all of history! And yet Christianity is quickly fading away in America.

Why is this happening? As referenced in Psalm 11:3, "If the foundations are destroyed, what can the righteous do?" There has been a foundational shift in our culture from God's Word as the authority to man's. This transformation did not happen overnight. It occurred in much the same way a person is carried by the ocean's tide when playing in the waves. One moment you're having a great time, and the next you look up and don't even recognize where you're at.

BIBLE REF.
Psalm 11:3
Matthew 7:24–27
Colossians 2:8
Jude 1:3

If the foundations are destroyed,
What can the righteous do?

But what allowed this steady erosion of biblical authority in the American culture? A loss of biblical authority within much of the church. The concession of biblical truth, especially in regard to origins, allowed the infiltration of secular ideas into the church. The culture has invaded the pews. Like Israel of old, the church has adopted doctrines of the current pagan religion, leaving it impotent to influence the surrounding culture. And like Israel of old, the first order of business must be repentance inside the church before there can be influence outside the church.

Why the division over creation **vs.** evolution?

Many Christians believe there is no need to quarrel over creation vs. evolution. They say, "Christians have lots of different views on other subjects, like baptism, tongues, eschatology, etc. Can't Christians have different views on origins?"

The short answer? No. And here's why. For the most part, when Christians have different understandings or interpretations of a particular doctrine, they stay within Scripture. Take eschatology, for example. There are lots of different views: pre-mil, post-mil, a-mil, wind-mil, tread-mil, etc. And in most instances, the people who hold to these different positions view Scripture as the authority for their positions. They're comparing Daniel with Ezekiel and Revelation to try to rightly understand God's Word. They're using the best commentary on the Bible, which is the Bible!

But this is **not** how Christians arrive at different views of origins. The way Christians get different understandings of Genesis is by reinterpreting it with ideas **outside** of the Bible. Imposing **secular** ideas like evolution, the presupposition the earth is millions of years old, uniformitarianism, and naturalism (all tenets of the **pagan religion** of humanism) *onto* the Bible results in things like The Day Age Theory, Gap Theory, Progressive Creation, Theistic Evolution, Framework Hypothesis, Cosmic Temple, etc.

BIBLE REF.
Ephesians 4:13–15
Romans 16:17
Romans 5:12
2 Timothy 3:16

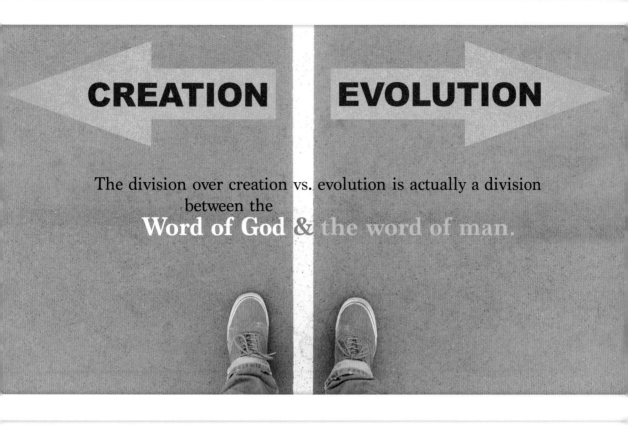

CREATION **EVOLUTION**

The division over creation vs. evolution is actually a division between the Word of God & the word of man.

All of these compromised ideas lead to major textual, doctrinal, and theological contradictions, as we'll see later on. This bending, editing, and manipulating of the Word of God is a failed attempt to make it bow to the word of fallible, finite, sinful man.

The division over creation vs. evolution is actually a division between the Word of God and the word of man. Either God's Word is true or man's word becomes the final authority.

Indeed, the body of Christ is to be unified (Ephesians 4:13–15), but that unity is founded upon the explicit truth of Scripture (Romans 16:17, 2 Timothy 3:16). Will Christians stand united on God's Word, trusting that the Creator of the universe can communicate effectively? Will we believe the account of origins clearly articulated in Genesis, affirmed by Jesus and the biblical authors, and confirmed by science?

Biblical authority

If you took a stethoscope and listened to the heartbeat of our ministry, Answers in Genesis (AiG), what would you hear? Biblical authority. We often share that AiG is not a creation vs. evolution ministry. AiG is about reaching our lost world and building up the faith of Christians by defending the authority of God's Word where it's being attacked today.

There is no doubt the Bible is under a barrage of assaults today. And one of the primary areas where the enemy has focused his attack is against the Bible's history. Particularly the history revealed in Genesis 1-11.

In a real sense, the devil has executed a covert attack on the foundation of God's Word by getting people to doubt the history of the Bible, with things like evolution, ape-men, big bang, millions of years, etc., to undermine the authority of the Bible, to ultimately undermine the Gospel that's based on that authority.

Therefore, we strive to alert believers to the present-day attack and encourage Christians and the Church at large to heed the command of 1 Peter 3:15:

"But sanctify the Lord God in your hearts, and always be ready to give a defense to everyone who asks you a reason for the hope that is in you, with meekness and fear."

It is this theme that pulses through AiG's veins, whether we're talking about the state-of-the-art Creation Museum, the

BIBLE REF.
Genesis 1-11
John 3:16
John 17:17
Titus 1:9
1 Peter 3:15

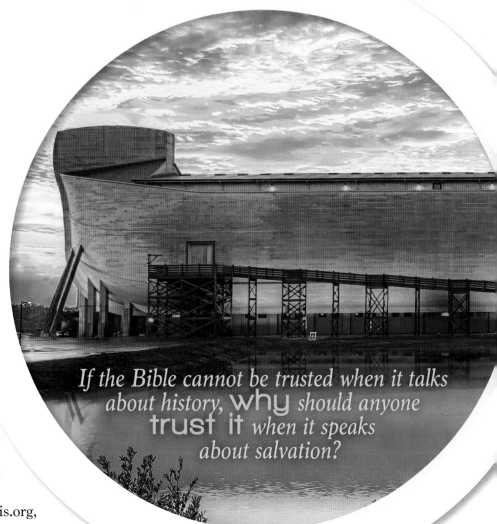

If the Bible cannot be trusted when it talks about history, **why** *should anyone* **trust it** *when it speaks about salvation?*

phenomenal Ark Encounter, our website at answersingenesis.org, our chronological ABC Sunday School curriculum, our world-traveling speakers, our books, our videos, or our curricula, etc.

All of it is dedicated to fighting on the front lines of the modern battle to promote the authority of God's Word, answering the skeptical questions of this age, demonstrating that God's Word is true from cover to cover, and leading to the powerful proclamation of the Gospel.

Bottom line: if the Bible cannot be trusted when it talks about history, why should anyone trust it when it speaks about salvation? If Genesis 1:1 is not true, neither is John 3:16.

It's an issue of authority.

2 Worldviews: God's vs. man's

Quite possibly the biggest misconception about the origins debate, by both creationists and evolutionists alike, is that it is a battle over who has the largest pile of evidence. The creationists are accumulating their pile of evidence, while the evolutionists are making their own pile of evidence, and the one with the largest pile in the end is the grand winner.

But the shocking truth is the real battle is over the same evidence! The same evidence that exists in the **present**.

Quick question: When do fossils exist, past or present? They exist in the present; if they didn't, we would not have any. And when someone finds a bone in the dirt, it does not come with a label disclosing its age. Nor do bones talk. If a bone talks to you, run away (or seek out the necessary medical attention)! When a fossil bone is discovered in the present, all that is known for sure is that something has died in the past.

Here is the point. All scientists today, whether secular or biblical, have the same facts in the **present**. The same rock layers, fossils, radioisotopes, DNA, stars in the sky, etc. But they get extremely different **interpretations** of what they are looking at in regard to the **unseen past** based on their different starting assumptions based on their different **worldviews** (religions). And as we'll see, secular scientists have reached really wrong conclusions about certain things

BIBLE REF.
1 Corinthians 1:20
2 Corinthians 10:5
2 Timothy 2:25

Those who trust man's guesses over God's Word assume the way things happen in nature now is the way they have always happened.

— like the age of the earth, rock layers, fossils, dinosaurs, etc. — because they have started with the wrong, anti-biblical worldview.

For those who start with the Bible, they use biblical history — the eyewitness account of the Creator Himself — to understand what is observed in the present.

Those who trust man's guesses over God's Word assume the way things happen in nature now is the way they have always happened. **Before** addressing the evidence, they **assume** no divine intervention in the past, no supernatural Creation, no Fall of man, no global Flood, no Tower of Babel, etc. They **assume** the Bible is wrong and believe by **faith** that natural processes can explain everything.

In the end, the battle over creation vs. evolution is a clash of worldviews. A struggle between the only two fundamental religions: man's word vs. God's Word.

EVOLUTION CREATION

What is the ultimate and supreme starting point?

So, if this issue of origins is a war of worldviews, then which worldview is the correct starting point?

A powerful initial argument would be that the biblical worldview is constantly confirmed by real science and evolutionism (humanism/atheism/materialism) is not. This will be seen over and over again throughout this book. The features of the rock layers, fossils, dinosaur tissue, DNA, etc., provide tremendous confirmations of the Bible's history and authenticity.

But here is the ultimate confirmation that the Word of God is the supreme starting point: only the biblical worldview can self-consistently make sense of all of reality. The biblical world-view alone can explain the origin of all things, material and immaterial alike, without contradicting itself.

The Bible provides the only logical explanation for all material things, like stars, planets, DNA, animals, and so on. But beyond that, the Bible provides the only coherent reason for the existence of non-material things, like the laws of logic, laws of nature, and absolute morality. Things that cannot be seen, tasted, or touched but are absolutely real.

BIBLE REF.
Proverbs 1:7
John 4:24
Colossians 2:3

These immaterial realities must be true for us to live, think, and operate within this world but make absolutely no sense without the biblical God. The all-powerful Creator of everything, seen and unseen, who has revealed Himself to us through His Word is the One who made man in His image so that mankind may understand and function within the universe He created.

The biblical worldview *alone can explain the* origin *of all things, material and immaterial alike,* without contradicting *itself.*

Only the biblical worldview can account for all of reality consistently. Every other worldview will eventually blow itself up by its own standard. Every worldview outside of the biblical one is "suicidal."

For example, the atheistic/evolutionary view is that everything is material. If it is not material (not physical), then they claim it doesn't exist. God is not material but Spirit (John 4:24), so they claim God doesn't exist because He is not material. See how that works? Now, likewise, love, truth, knowledge, logic, dignity, honor, and so on are also not material. So, in the atheistic view, these cannot exist, either! Of course, this causes a big problem! The atheist, by his own worldview, cannot make sense of a discussion about anything without jumping off his worldview and waving good-bye to it!

Or consider the currently popular worldview of relativism, the belief that everything is relative and there are **no absolute** truths. But are they **absolutely** sure? For them to be right, they must be wrong. That's what is meant by suicidal.

And because of the suicidal nature of all non-biblical worldviews, all of them must borrow from the biblical one to operate within reality. Ironically, those who reject and argue against the Bible must use principles that only exist because the Bible is true!

A Perfect Creation

Why do Bible-believers believe creation?

Christians are instructed to build all of their thinking on the foundation of God's Word by taking every thought captive and making it obedient to Christ (2 Corinthians 10:5).

Therefore, Bible-believers believe in creation first and foremost because that is what the Bible plainly reveals.

In Job 38:4, God asks Job a rhetorical question, "Where were you when I laid the foundation of the earth? Tell Me, if you have understanding." The point? God was there, and Job was not. As a matter of fact, no humans were there, but God was.

It is God Himself, the one who cannot lie (Titus 1:2), who knows everything (Psalm 147:5), who has always existed (Revelation 22:13), and who unveils the mystery of origins (Isaiah 46:10). In Genesis 1 and 2, God gives a clear historical account of His divine act of creation. In Exodus 20:11 and Exodus 31:17, He echoes this history as the foundation for the seven-day week and the fourth of the Ten Commandments. And it is worth remembering that God wrote the Ten Commandments with His own finger (Exodus 31:18)!

The Bible is the perfect eyewitness testimony of the Creator Himself! How could those who call Christ "Lord" not believe it? It is trustworthy in all it says because "All Scripture is breathed out by God and profitable for teaching, for reproof, for correction and for training in righteousness" (2 Timothy 3:16 ESV).

BIBLE REF.
Job 38:4
Psalm 147:5
Isaiah 46:10 2
Corinthians 10:5
Titus 1:2
Revelation 22:13

All Scripture is breathed out *by God and* profitable *for teaching, for reproof, for correction and for training in* righteousness.

2 Timothy 3:16

Christians are exhorted in the book of Psalms that the law of the Lord is perfect, His testimony trustworthy and a light to the believer's path (Psalm 19:7; 119:105). In Proverbs, it is declared that every word of God is flawless (Proverbs 30:5). There is also a warning given that every believer should take to heart: never add to or take away from God's words "or He will rebuke you and prove you a liar" (Proverbs 30:6, Deuteronomy 4:2, Revelation 22:18–19).

Why didn't God make the world perfect?

Actually, He did make it perfect. Today's world is a shattered representation of God's original creation (Romans 8:22). The Bible records in Genesis 1:31 that God declared at the end of day six of creation that all He had made was "very good." Of course, that begs the question of what is "good" to the perfect, all-knowing and all-powerful God? Answer: perfection. Logically, this should not be surprising. What else would one expect from a perfect God other than a perfect creation? Deuteronomy 32:4 states, "He is the Rock, **His work is perfect**; For all His ways are justice, a God of truth and without injustice; righteous and upright is He."

This original perfect creation was innocent, free of death and the curse, which were both the consequences of man's sin (Genesis 3, Romans 5, 8; 1 Corinthians 15). Death, suffering, and disease were by no means part of God's flawless creation. This means, among other things, that in the initial creation everything was vegetarian. This is clarified explicitly in Genesis 1:29–30 when God tells Adam and Eve to eat fruit and everything with the breath of life to eat plants.

If one thinks about it, this makes perfect biblical sense. The Bible is clear from beginning to end that death is an enemy, the consequence of sin. Which means there could not have been any meat-eating until **after** Adam's sin because there

BIBLE REF.

Genesis 1:29–31
Genesis 9:3
Deuteronomy 32:4
Romans 5
Romans 8:22

This original perfect creation was
innocent,
free of death and the curse,
which were both the consequences of man's sin.

was **no death** until **after** Adam's sin. It was not until after the Flood that God allowed man to eat meat (Genesis 9:3).

Of course, everything changed when sin entered the world. But that does not change the fact that in the beginning God made a perfect creation and there is the glorious restoration to perfection when Christ returns (Revelation 21–22)!

Six days... why?
And really?

"God is all-powerful, He could have created over millions of years, right?" Of course, but the question is not what God could have done; rather, it is what did He say He did. And as the believer takes an honest look at the creation account in Genesis 1, the clarity of what God said He did is overwhelming, and the question then becomes "Will we take God at His Word?"

First, the construction of the Hebrew language used in Genesis 1 plainly reveals that it is historical narrative (recorded history). It is not poetic; it is not allegory or metaphor. Even Jesus quoted it as literal history in Matthew 19:4–5 and Mark 10:6. Throughout the Bible, subsequent writers treated the early chapters of Genesis as literal history.[1]

Hebrew scholars, both Christian and secular, often point out that, based on the context and language, Genesis is literal historical narrative.[2]

Second, the Hebrew word for day is *yôm*, and like its English counterpart, it has various meanings depending on **context**. Essentially, every time in the Old Testament the word yôm is accompanied by a number, the words "evening and/or morning," or by the word "night," it means a **literal,**

BIBLE REF.
Genesis 1
Exodus 20:11
Matthew 19:4–5
Mark 10:6

1 Terry Mortenson, "Did Bible Authors Believe in a Literal Genesis?", *The Answers Book 3*, ed. Ken Ham (Green Forest, AR: Master Books, 2010), pp. 81–90.
2 For example, see Dr. Donald B. DeYoung, *Thousands, Not Billions* (Green Forest, AR: Master Books, 2005), p. 168; see also Oxford Hebrew scholar and professor James Barr on the meaning of Genesis: James Barr, letter to David C. C. Watson, April 23, 1984, https://answersingenesis.org/genesis/oxford-hebrew-scholar-professor-james-barr-meaning-of-genesis/.

Throughout the Bible*, subsequent writers treated the early chapters of Genesis as* literal history *including* Jesus.

24-hour day.[3] In Genesis

1, at the end of each day, this phrase/context is observed, "there was evening and morning, the first day" (ESV). It is clear from the context of Genesis 1 that the days of Creation Week were six literal, 24-hour days.

As if that wasn't enough, Exodus 20:11 states without equivocation, "For in six days the Lord made the heavens and the earth, the sea, and all that is in them."

3 Jim Stambaugh, "The Days of Creation: A Semantic Approach," Answers in Genesis, April 1, 1991, https://answersingenesis.org/days-of-creation/the-days-of-creation-a-semantic-approach/.

How old
is the earth?

So, what is the age of the earth according to the Bible? Well, it first must be understood that nowhere in the Bible does it directly state the earth is 6,000 years old. Which is good, because the Bible was written roughly 2,000–3,500 years ago, and if it had stated then that the earth was 6,000 years old, it would have been wrong! Nor did Moses, or any other author, state the age of the earth at the time of their writings. Again, that's a very good thing because if they did, what they wrote would be wrong the very next day.

What the Bible does give us is so much better. In a sense, what is recorded in the pages of Scripture is a "birth certificate" for the earth and universe — a way of accurately identifying the birthdate of the universe and calculating the age based on that information.

What is this "birth certificate"? Genesis 1:1! The earth and universe were created at the beginning on the first day (Genesis 1:1-5). Then we pick up with the biblical genealogies (the family trees of the Bible that effectively combat insomnia!), especially those found in Genesis 5 and 11. In these genealogies, the age of the father is given at the time of the son's birth: "Adam lived one hundred and thirty years, and begot . . . Seth. . . . Seth lived one hundred and five years, and begot Enosh. . . . Enosh lived ninety years, and begot Cainan" (Genesis 5:3-9).

BIBLE REF.
Genesis 1:1
Genesis 1:1-5
Genesis 5:3-9

What is recorded in the pages of Scripture is a **"birth certificate"** *for the earth and universe.*

One need only to add these ages up — it's not hard to do — to get an accurate estimate for the age of the earth.

From Adam to Abraham, it's approximately 2,000 years (technically the earth, which was made on day one, is five days older than Adam, who was made on day six), from Abraham to Christ is about 2,000 years and from Christ to today is roughly 2,000 years. Put all that together, and the simple math clearly implies the earth was created around 4,000 B.C. (or 6,000 years ago from today). Believe it or not, most chronologists of the Old Testament, Jewish or Christian, have tabulated dates near this for the past 2,000 years!

Radiometric dating?

But doesn't radiometric dating prove the earth is millions of years old? Not in the least. Actually, most dating techniques point to a very young earth, and only a few of the radiometric dating methods used suggest an old earth.

And it cannot be overstated that no one looks at isotopes and measures age. Secularists look at ratios and conversions of isotopes in the **present**, make a whole host of unknown, naturalistic (anti-biblical and, therefore, not neutral) **assumptions** and extrapolate backwards in time to make a **guess** about an age. Here's a quick look at the assumptions that drive the conclusion of millions of years.

Secularists today assume **uniformitarianism**, an idea that the present is the key to the past. The way things happen now is the way they have always happened in the unobserved past (i.e., no catastrophes occurred in the past — like a global Flood). For example, they assume that isotope rates of decay, observed for less than a hundred years, have been the same for millions or billions of years into the past.

This is a gigantic, unverifiable, **faith-based** assumption. It's a faith based on the worldview of **naturalism** (nature is all there is), the religion veraciously proselytized by the secularist. They are assuming, out of hand, no special creation or global Flood as clearly described in the Bible. These events would likely affect the initial amounts of elements within a

BIBLE REF.
Proverbs 12:1
Proverbs 23:12

If we can't trust isotope dating when dating rocks of known age, *how is it plausible to trust it when dating rocks of* unknown age?

rock, the decay rate, contamination, etc. Thus, they are **assuming** the Bible is wrong, which explicitly reveals that they are not neutral when evaluating the Biblical claims.

On top of that, when we date rocks of known age, isotope dating consistently gives wildly inaccurate dates! Examples are legion, so let's take a look at one. Remember Mount St. Helens, a volcano that erupted twice in the early 1980s? The lava dome expanded and finally cooled and solidified into rock in 1986 (this was supposed to start the radiometric dating "clock"), but when these rocks were then dated with potassium-argon dating in the early 2000s, they were dated as high as 2.8 million years old![1]

So, if we can't trust isotope dating when dating rocks of known age, how is it plausible to trust it when dating rocks of unknown age?

1 Keith Swenson, "Radio-Dating in Rubble," Answers in Genesis, June 1, 2001, https://answersingenesis.org/geology/radiometric-dating/radio-dating-in-rubble/.

Carbon dating?

A great example of the unreliability of radiometric dating is carbon dating. Using this method, one part of the Vollosovitch mammoth dated at **29,500** years and another part **44,000**[1]. That's a slow birth! Freshly killed seals were dated at 1,300 years, and other seals dead for no longer than 30 years were dated at 4,600 years.[2]

As a matter of fact, carbon 14 dating turns out to be one of the best evidences for a young earth! Here's how. Carbon 14 is an unstable element that forms in the atmosphere from nitrogen and is absorbed by plants in the form of carbon dioxide (only the carbon is carbon 14). Animals then eat the plants, and people eat both plants and animals. As a result, carbon 14 resides in all organisms. When an organism dies, it stops taking in carbon 14. Carbon 14, being unstable, will change into nitrogen 14 fairly quickly due to its rapid decay rate. Actually, carbon 14 decays so quickly that within 100,000 years (as calculations reveal) after an organism's death, no detectable carbon 14 should be left in an organism's remnants.

Not that carbon 14 dating is accurate, but its maximum theoretical date-implications are clear and powerful. Any organic fossil remnant that is supposedly older than 100,000 years should have no measurable carbon 14. So, what do we actually find with observable science? Essentially, all organic remnants, like

1 Troy L Pewe, "Quaternary Stratigraphic Nomenclature in Unglaciated Central Alaska," United States Geological Survey, Geological Survey Professional Paper 862 (1975): p. 30.
2 Wakefield Dort. Jr., "Mummified Seals of Southern Victoria Land," *Antarctic Journal of the United States* (June 1971): p. 210.

Carbon 14 dating turns out to be one of the
best evidences
for a young earth!

coal and diamond, in all rock layers,
no matter their evolutionary-assumed age,
contain large amounts of carbon 14. Fantastic forensic proof that all
those remnants and all those rock layers are only thousands of years old
— no way millions. This evidence is strong confirmation of the truth of
biblical history and a firm rejection of evolutionary geology.

Dinosaurs were made on day 6?

So, if the earth is only thousands of years old as the Bible plainly implies and observable science confirms, then what about the dinosaurs!? For many years now, dinosaurs have been a mystery to most Christians because of the influence of evolutionary thinking in our culture and churches. But when we start with the Bible and build our thinking on God's Word, we have answers even about dinosaurs!

Answers in Genesis uses the "7 F's" to summarize dinosaurs from a biblical perspective.

1. **Formed** – The Bible states clearly that land animals were created on day six. Therefore, dinosaurs (land animals by definition) were formed on day six.

2. **Fearless** – God's initial creation was "very good." There was no death, suffering, or disease. Originally, everything was vegetarian, and there was no fear between animals and man.

3. **Fallen** – But then that all changed. Man sinned, bringing death and suffering into this world, and all of creation was affected (Romans 8:22). At this point, it is likely that the diets of many animals changed, and after the Flood, God put the fear of man into all the animals.

4. **Flood** – The global, catastrophic Flood of Noah's day killed all dinosaurs not on the Ark and buried many of their remains in rock layers all around the world. (Dinosaurs on the Ark!? Absolutely! This will be dealt with in a later chapter).

BIBLE REF.
Genesis 1:24–31
Genesis 6:13
Job 40:15-19
Romans 8:22

When we start with the Bible *and build our thinking on God's Word, we have* answers *even about* dinosaurs!

This is confirmed by the numerous samples of soft tissue discovered in dinosaur bones. At most, these tissues, with phenomenal preservation, would only last thousands of years after the dinosaur's death.

5. **Faded** — After the Flood, dinosaurs repopulated and lived with man for quite a while. This is firmly attested to by the thousands of images and writings of cultures worldwide that clearly depict dinosaurs. Bear in mind, that the word dinosaur is a new word. It was invented in 1841 by Sir Richard Owen and wasn't used much until the early 1900s. Before that time, dinosaurs would have been included in the groups of animals called "dragons." But the post-Flood world provided challenges to survival that the dinosaurs could not handle: it was a wrecked world (Genesis 6:13), genetic bottleneck, post-Flood Ice Age, man hunting them, etc. As a result, the land dragons, later renamed dinosaurs, faded away until all that was left were the legends that grew more fanciful as they were passed from one generation to the next in different cultures.

6. **Found** — Dinosaurs were rediscovered in the 1800s and were renamed by Sir Richard Owen. Actually, the first man to discover a dinosaur was . . . Adam.

7. **Fiction** — Since their rediscovery, there has been quite a bit of fabrication as to where dinosaurs came from and where they went, and the secular story that they existed millions of years before man is simply fiction.

A Corrupt Creation

Death before sin?

From the ministry's experience, this is one of the primary areas where many Christians (including, for years, the authors) have not thought this through to its logical, theological conclusion.

Here's the problem in a nutshell. No matter what idea a Christian may use to attempt to squeeze millions of years into the Bible — day age, progressive creation, gap theory, theistic evolution, cosmic temple, framework hypothesis, etc. — they all have this fatal flaw: all of them put millions of years of death before sin, which is a theological impossibility.

The Bible is explicitly clear, from cover to cover, that death is the consequence of sin (Genesis 1:29–30, Genesis 2:17, Genesis 3, Romans 5:12, 1 Corinthians 15:21–22).[1] Death is described as an enemy, the last enemy to be destroyed (1 Corinthians 15:26, Revelation 20:14). But if millions of years were true, death existed long before man or sin, which would make God the author of death who looked down on day six after millions of years of death, suffering, and diseases, and called everything "very good" (Genesis 1:31).

This clearly impugns the character of God. And if death was indeed part of God's original "very good" creation, then why would He describe it as the enemy that would one day be

BIBLE REF.
Genesis 2:17
Genesis 3
Romans 5:12
1 Corinthians 15:21–22
Revelation 20:14

---

1 Even animal death has a relationship to human sin. The first recorded death of an animal in the Bible is in Genesis 3:21, which was a direct result of human sin. Animals were often sacrificed to cover man's sin throughout the Old Testament and were a shadow of the things to come in Christ. In other words, these animal sacrifices point to Christ's [the Lamb of God's] final and ultimate sacrifice.

The Bible is **explicitly clear,** *from cover to cover, that* **death** *is the* consequence *of* **sin.**

destroyed? On top of that, the future hope of the Christian is that one day God will restore the world to its "pre-fall" state. But if there were millions of years of death and suffering before man existed, then what will God restore the world to? More death and suffering?

Most important of all, death is presented as the payment for sin (Hebrews 9:22, Leviticus 17:11, Romans 6:23, 1 Peter 2:24). But if you have millions of years and death before sin, then death is not the payment for sin.

And if death is not the payment for sin, then Jesus' death does not pay our sin debt, and we are all still lost in our sins and bound for hell!

Thus, the doctrines of atonement and salvation utterly collapse. That's why the issue of the age of the earth is, ultimately, a core, foundational issue and not a side issue. And that's why we at AiG are so passionate about defending the authority of God's Word and the gospel that's based in that authority where it's under assault today!

Why is there death and suffering?

It's interesting; one of Darwin's chief arguments against the biblical God is consistently echoed by aggressive atheists today. The general sentiment is this: there is no way a good and all-powerful God made a world like this. A world full of death and suffering, "red in tooth and claw," full of deadly catastrophes and diseases like cancer and Alzheimer's.

Ironically, they are right. Did God make a world like this? No. As stated previously, God made a "very good," perfect creation. So, what happened? Man wrecked this world through sin. And one shouldn't blame the manufacturer for the perfectly good car the driver wrecked. God's Word is clear when it states in Romans 5:12, "Therefore, just as through one man sin entered the world, and death through sin, and thus death spread to all men, because all sinned" (see also Genesis 3:17–19, 1 Corinthians 15:21).

It is because of man's sin that death and the curse invaded God's flawless creation, resulting in bloodshed, suffering, thorns, natural catastrophes, horrific diseases, etc. And that sin affected everything: "For we know that the whole creation groans and labors with birth pangs together until now" (Romans 8:22).

All of creation was cursed and looks forward to the coming consummation when it will be returned to its original perfection (Revelation 21:4).

BIBLE REF.
Genesis 3:17–19
Romans 5:12
Romans 8:22
1 Corinthians 15:21
Revelation 21:4

So, within the biblical worldview, the origin of death and suffering is accounted for, and victory over death is provided through God's plan of salvation. In the end, death will be destroyed, and God's perfect kingdom will remain established forever (1 Corinthians 15:26, Revelation 20:14).

Just as through one man sin entered the world, and death through sin, *and thus death spread to all men, because all sinned.* Romans 5:12

But how does the atheist account for his angst towards death and suffering? Within his worldview, these things are merely properties of a random and meaningless universe. The fact that he finds these things troubling suggests an absolute moral standard by which to call certain things evil and others good. But that absolute standard can only exist if there is a perfect, infinite, eternal, transcendent God who sets that standard. Whether he realizes it or not, the atheist is borrowing from the Christian worldview.

Should Christians believe millions of years?

So, should Christians believe in millions of years? Well, based on what's already been said, it's safe to say the answer is a resounding no. We saw earlier the grammar of Genesis and sound biblical theology slam the proverbial door in the face of the naturalistic myth of millions of years.

Here are a few other reasons millions of years and Genesis are irreconcilable.

Local Flood: Embracing millions of years essentially means one must accept that Noah's Flood was just a local event, completely against the clear meaning of the text (more on this later).

Day Age Theory: If each day of creation was an age of time, that presents its own unique problems. For example, plants were made on day three and the sun on day four. But if day three was millions of years long, that means plants would have to survive for millions of years without the sun!

Timing Issues: The order in which things were created in the Bible is practically the opposite of the order suggested by evolutionists. So, just adding millions of years to the biblical account will not reconcile the two.

Gap Theory: One, the Hebrew grammar of Genesis 1:1-2 will not allow for it. Two, it is suggested that during this supposed gap between Genesis 1:1 and 1:2 is when Satan fell and corrupted the world, there was a global flood called "Lucifer's Flood," and there may have

BIBLE REF.
Genesis 1:1-2
Genesis 1:31
Proverbs 9:10

Millions of years is based on an atheistic interpretation *of rocks, fossils, isotopes, and history.*

been a pre-Adamite race of soulless hominids. Of course, the Bible never mentions a pre-Adamite race or "Lucifer's Flood." If Satan/Lucifer fell on day one, then that would make Satan and sin "very good!" One can make a solid biblical argument that Satan did not fall until after God's declaration that everything was very good (Genesis 1:31) and surely after day seven of creation week (a day that God sanctified and made holy).

Besides all that (and much more could be said), the idea of millions of years is based on an atheistic interpretation of rocks, fossils, isotopes, and history. Millions of years was conceived from and is part of the **religion** of naturalism, a form of humanism. Truly, is there any legitimate reason for a Christian to follow the example of the Old Testament Israelites and try to squeeze another religion into God's Word?

Where did Cain get his wife?

This question is a classic. In 1925, William Jennings Bryan was asked this very question in the famous "Scopes Monkey Trial" in Dayton, Tennessee. He didn't have an answer then, and unfortunately many believers do not have an answer now.

The question goes like this. Adam and Eve had Cain and Abel, Cain kills Abel, and Cain went off and had a family with his wife. But where did Cain get his wife (Genesis 4:1–17)? Well, the Bible is clear that Adam was the first man (1 Corinthians 15:45), Eve is the "mother of all living" (Genesis 3:20), and all humans are of "one blood" (Acts 17:26). The fact that all people are descendants of Adam and Eve means there is only one biological race, and it's also the reason we're all sinners in need of a Savior.

So, what's the answer? It's closer than one might think. Just flip the page of the Bible to Genesis 5:4 where it is recorded, "After he begot Seth, the days of Adam were eight hundred years; and he had sons and **daughters**." Jewish tradition suggests that Adam and Eve had thirty-three sons and twenty-three daughters.[1] That means, originally, brothers married sisters.

Wait, can you marry your relation? Yes, no, probably, only after counseling? The answer is actually *yes*; if you don't marry your relation, then you're not marrying a human, and you've really got problems! Abraham was married to his half-sister, and it was not an issue. It wasn't until the time of Moses, 2,500 years

BIBLE REF.
Genesis 3:20
Genesis 4:1–17
Genesis 5:4
Leviticus 18:6
Acts 17:26

---

1 Josephus, *The Works of Josephus: Complete and Unabridged*, trans. William Whiston (Peabody, MA: Hendrickson Publishers, Inc, 1987) p. 32 (93 AD Josephus; 1736 AD Whiston).

Adam and Eve were genetically **perfect**, *preprogrammed straight from the* **hand of God**.

Image from the Scopes Trial

after creation, in the book of Leviticus, when God prohibited marrying a close relative (Leviticus 18:6).

But why was marrying a close relative originally okay and later on forbidden by God? One of the reasons people don't marry close relatives today is because humans have thousands of years of accumulated mutations (damaged genetic information) within their genome/DNA. If someone marries a close relative, it is probable both of them will have common mutations, which, if passed on by both parties, will likely end up as a birth defect. So, a person marries someone further away in relation to get good genes to mask bad genes and help prevent the expressing of birth defects.

But, initially, this was not a problem. Adam and Eve were genetically perfect, preprogrammed straight from the hand of God. Even when they sinned and mutations came on the scene as a result of the curse, those mutations would have been few in number for quite a while. So, originally, it would have been no problem to marry a close relative until those mutations accumulated to a detrimental point, and that's when God stepped in.

A Catastrophic Flooded Creation

Rock layers–millions of years or a global Flood?

Either most of the rock layers were laid down slowly and are evidence for millions of years, or they were deposited catastrophically and are dynamic testimony of Noah's Flood. It should be immediately obvious that these two interpretations are mutually exclusive. If one says "both!", then the Flood would have destroyed the previous layers and laid down new ones! So, which explanation do the features of the rock layers confirm?

1. Rock layers around the world cover large portions of continents or even multiple continents. (Best explained by the Flood)

2. Between the rock layers, there is no evidence of slow erosion, soil, or topography. (Confirms the Flood)

3. In these rock layers, fossilized tracks, ripples, and raindrops are found. These features only form on soft sediment and would only be preserved by rapid burial by another layer of sediment. (Confirms the Flood)

4. Fossilized tracks tend to go up through the rock layers with the actual fossilized critter found in a "higher" rock layer, implying the critter is trying to avoid burial as rock layers were being deposited quickly during the Flood. (Confirms the Flood)

5. There is practically no evidence of bioturbation (evidence of life) within the rock layers. (Confirms the Flood)

BIBLE REF.
Genesis 6–8
Psalm 104:8–9

Author Bryan Osborne beside the Tapeats Sandstone in the eastern Grand Canyon.

6. All over the world, multiple rock layers are curved and bent, sometimes dramatically, in the same direction, strongly implying they were laid down around the same time and then bent all together while still wet. (Confirms the Flood)

7. Polystrate fossils are found around the world. These are fossils that go through multiple rock layers. This is a real problem if one believes those layers are millions of years old. (Confirms the Flood)

8. We observe billions of dead things called fossils buried in these rock layers that were laid down by water all over the earth. But dead things do not turn to fossils unless they are catastrophically and rapidly buried to protect them from oxygen, bacteria, and scavengers. (Confirms the Flood)

Two other quick things: First, due to the moving waters of Noah's Flood, one would expect sediment particles (clay, sand, gravel, etc.) to settle in distinct layers based on size, weight, density, and circumference. This is a well-observed phenomenon called Hydrodynamic Sorting.

Second, rocks do not take millions of years to form. All that is required is water, sediment, and chemicals, and minerals and rocks can form quickly. Attesting to this, a ship's bell, an ancient clock, and a spark plug have been found encased in rock.[1] Also, the effects of the eruption of Mount St. Helens produced hundreds of rock layers, as well as canyons in only hours or days. All of this is great observational evidence that it does not take millions of years to make rock layers (or canyons), just a catastrophe. And to get bigger rock layers, all that's needed is a bigger catastrophe, like Noah's Flood!

1 Dr. John Whitmore, "Aren't Millions of Years Required for Geological Processes?", Answers in Genesis, July 15, 2010, https://answersingenesis.org/geology/arent-millions-of-years-required-for-geological-processes/.

Flood: local or global?

Another unavoidable consequence of Christians embracing millions of years is one must believe that Noah's Flood was just a local event. Why? Because the idea of millions of years is built upon the naturalist assumption that the rock layers were laid down slowly over eons of time.

But that would mean Noah's Flood could not have been global, such an event would have ripped up all those rock layers thousands of years ago and laid down its own sediment layers. So, Noah's Flood could have only flooded Noah's little universe, the Mesopotamian valley (basically modern-day Iraq). Unfortunately, many churches, Christian schools, Bible colleges, and seminaries teach a local Flood because they have compromised on the millions of years.

The problems with this idea are legion; here are a few.

As already discussed, clear biblical exposition does not allow for millions of years, and the features of the rock record emphatically confirm the global Flood.

If the Flood was only a local event, here are some good questions:

1. Why have Noah build an Ark? God could have just told him to move.

2. Why send animals, especially birds, to the Ark? They could have easily avoided "a local flood." If not, there would still be plenty to repopulate.

BIBLE REF.
Genesis 6:13, 17
Genesis 7:21–23
Genesis 7:19–20
Genesis 9:8–17

Clear **biblical** *exposition does not allow for millions of* **years**, *and the features of the rock record emphatically* **confirm** *the* **global** *Flood.*

3. Why make the Ark so big (over 100,000 sq. ft.!) for only local critters?

4. What about all the people who were not living in the vicinity of the Flood? They would have escaped God's judgment.

Most important, what does Scripture say? In Genesis 6:13, 17, God declares His purpose for the Flood, "I am going to put an end to *all* people. . . . I am surely going to destroy both them and the earth. . . . I am going to bring floodwaters on the earth to destroy *all* life under the heavens. . . . *Everything* on earth will perish" (NIV). Genesis 7:21–23 confirms God's prediction.

During the Flood, the Bible reports that everything under the heavens was covered by water, and the highest mountains by 20 feet of water, which would be impossible if it was not global (Genesis 7:19–20). It's worth mentioning that the other biblical authors and Jesus Himself viewed the Flood as an all-encompassing event.

Also, the rainbow was a sign of God's promise to never again send a flood as He did in the days of Noah (Genesis 9:8–17). But if the Flood was a local event, then God has broken His promise several times over.

Could Noah hold all those animals on the Ark?

As speakers for Answers in Genesis, we get this question a lot, and we tend to respond with two questions of our own:

1. How big was the Ark?

2. How many animals did Noah actually take?

The answers to these two questions are the key to the answer of this common question by the skeptics. So, let's take them in turn.

1. How big was the Ark?

Based on the dimensions given in Genesis 6:15, the Ark was approximately 510 feet long, 85 feet wide, and 51 feet tall (using the long cubit). Interestingly enough, those are the same proportions of many modern day cargo ships (It's like God knew what He was doing). Inside the Ark were three different levels. It had capacity equally to roughly 570 railroad stock cars. It was literally a floating warehouse with well over 100,000 square feet. But was it big enough?

2. How many animals did Noah actually take?

The Bible states clearly that Noah only took pairs (in some cases seven) of land-dwelling, air-breathing animals onto the Ark (Genesis 6:19–20). No fish! Plenty of water outside the boat.

Also, it is very likely Noah brought young adults onto the Ark (e.g., less food, less waste, less space, etc.). Perhaps most important of all, the Bible says Noah took two of each kind, not two of each species (Genesis 6:19–20). In most cases the biblical

BIBLE REF.
Genesis 6:15
Genesis 6:19–20

kind seems roughly equal to the family level of modern-day classification. As an example, Noah did not take hundreds of different dogs onto the Ark. He probably never saw a Chihuahua or Poodle in his life! He just took two of the dog kind.

So, how many kinds would Noah need to account for all the variations we see today and in the fossil record? At most, about 1,400. Taking two of each and seven of some (i.e., clean animals, which was a small list in the Bible), the probable total was around 4,000, with a maximum, worst-case scenario being approximately 7,000 (the number we are using for the Ark Encounter). Plenty of room on the Ark for all the necessary animals, Noah, his family, food, and supplies. The real question is: why did he build an Ark with so much leftover space?

Originally one continent?

In Genesis 1:9 God commands, "Let the water under the sky be gathered to one place, and let dry ground appear" (NIV). If the water was in "one place," it would make sense that the land likely was in "one place." It is then very probable that there was originally one major supercontinent, like Pangea or Rodinia, that existed before the Flood.

What happened to that supercontinent? The Flood of Noah's day! Genesis 7:11–12 states, "On that day **all** the **springs of the great deep burst forth**, and the floodgates of the heavens were opened" (NIV). The "springs of the great deep" refers to subterranean water, water underneath the surface of the earth. This is not weird— we find some of that today. And the Hebrew verb for "burst forth" is used in a couple of other places,[1] and in each case, it describes the ground of the earth cracking open and moving violently.

So, during the Flood, all over the world, the earth's continental crust was catastrophically broken open and rapidly moving. Today, when the earth's crust moves just a little, there are earthquakes, tsunamis, and volcanic activity. If that's what happens when the crust moves just a bit, what would happen if the crust of the earth was broken open all over the globe and moved dramatically? There would be earthquakes, tsunamis,

BIBLE REF.
Genesis 1:9
Genesis 6:13
Genesis 7:11–12

1 Numbers 16:31-33, Zechariah 14:4

Essentially, the Genesis Flood caused "continental sprint" *as opposed to the modern idea of slow and gradual* "continental drift."

and volcanic activity on an incomprehensible scale. It would be enough to destroy the world, part of the purpose of the Flood (Genesis 6:13).

Essentially, the Genesis Flood caused "continental sprint" as opposed to the modern idea of slow and gradual "continental drift." And as it turns out, to move a tectonic plate, a catastrophic process is required. Long, slow, gradual processes simply do not produce enough energy or the right conditions to move a tectonic plate, no matter how much time you give them.

Where did the water come from and where did it go?

Where did the water come from? According to the Bible, the water for the Flood came from two sources: from below the earth, "springs of the great deep," and above the earth, "floodgates of the heavens."

Where did it go? It's still here! The water from the Flood now resides predominantly in today's oceans and seas. Around three-quarters of the earth's surface is presently covered by water. And here's a little-known fact. If one were to press down the earth's mountain ranges just a bit and raise up the ocean basins just a bit, the entire world would be covered by approximately 1.6 miles of water right now!

Some Bible researchers believe the text indicates how God ended the Flood in Psalm 104:8-9: "The mountains rose; the valleys sank down" (ESV).

"The mountains rose": Toward the end of the Flood, new mountain ranges form because of all the tectonic activity taking place as a result of the "springs of the great deep burst forth." This explains a couple of things.

1. Some have argued that Noah's Flood could not have covered Mount Everest for numerous reasons. We agree! Because Mount Everest did not exist until the end of the Flood when "the mountains rose."

BIBLE REF.
Psalm 104:8-9

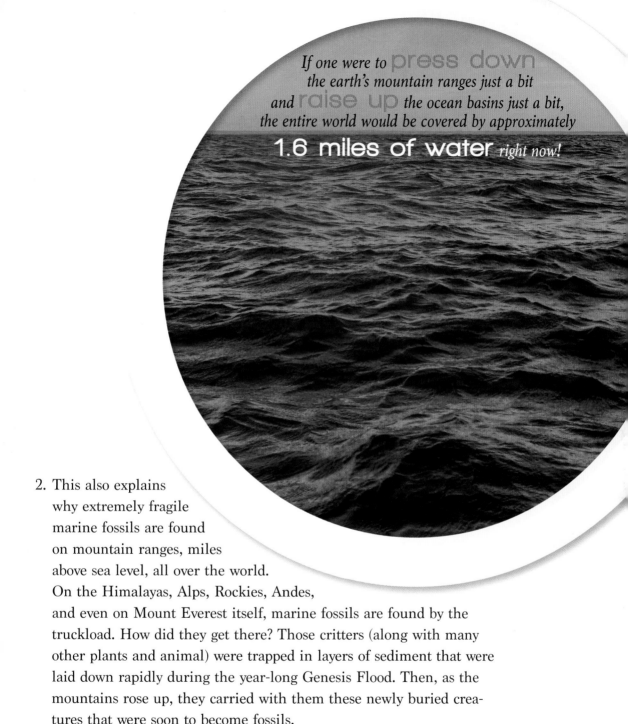

If one were to press down *the earth's mountain ranges just a bit* and raise up *the ocean basins just a bit, the entire world would be covered by approximately* **1.6 miles of water** *right now!*

2. This also explains why extremely fragile marine fossils are found on mountain ranges, miles above sea level, all over the world. On the Himalayas, Alps, Rockies, Andes, and even on Mount Everest itself, marine fossils are found by the truckload. How did they get there? Those critters (along with many other plants and animal) were trapped in layers of sediment that were laid down rapidly during the year-long Genesis Flood. Then, as the mountains rose up, they carried with them these newly buried creatures that were soon to become fossils.

"The valleys sank down": As the valleys sank down, the waters of Noah's Flood rushed into the newly formed ocean basins. As a result, massive erosion features are prominent all over the earth's land surface.

Dinosaurs on the Ark?

The Bible testifies that pairs of all creatures with the "breath of life" came to Noah and entered the Ark (Genesis 7:15). That means dinosaurs were on the Ark!

Some will argue, "But aren't there thousands of variations of dinosaurs?" There are many variations but not that many kinds. Just like there are many variations of the dog kind but just the one kind, the same is true for dinosaur kinds. There are many variations of the Ceratopsian kind (triceratops, protoceratops, torosaurus, etc.), but just the one Ceratopsid/Ceratopsian kind.

There are many variations of the sauropod kind (Brachiosaurus, Apatosaurus, etc.), but just the one sauropod kind. Being really generous, there are about 36 to 85 dinosaur kinds. And Noah took two of each kind, so that's only around 72 to 170 total dinosaurs!

But then some will argue, "Maybe there weren't that many, but dinosaurs were too big!" What most people don't realize is that the average size of a dinosaur was that of a bison. Some were as small as chickens. If they were still around, we could have some KFD (Kentucky Fried Dinosaurs)! Actually, all dinosaurs started off small because they hatched from eggs. And the biggest an egg can get is about the size of a football. That means all dinosaurs, whether you're talking about the T. rex, Stegosaurus, Apatosaurus, etc., all started off no bigger than the size of a football.

BIBLE REF.
Genesis 7:15
Genesis 8:19

Just like there are many variations of the **dog kind** *but just the one kind, the same is true for the variations of* **dinosaur kinds**.

With that in mind, it just makes sense that God would have brought juveniles of dinosaurs and other big animals onto the Ark. He would likely bring juveniles because they are smaller, eat less, weigh less, sleep more, and are a lot more resilient. Most importantly, juveniles will live longer once they get off the Ark, giving them more time to produce more offspring, which is the whole reason they were brought on board to begin with. Really, there is no problem getting dinosaurs on the Ark.

A Confused Creation

Why the Tower of Babel?

Like the rest of Genesis 1–11, the account of the Tower of Babel is under assault today and is vital in connecting what we see in God's world to what we read in God's Word.

To start with, many skeptics claim there is a contradiction between chapters 10 and 11. In chapter 10, it says the people were separated into their lands by their languages, and chapter 11 says they all spoke one language.

Actually, a similar argument against Genesis 1 and 2 is often employed by the doubter, but the solution in both cases is the same. Quite often, Hebrew narratives will give the summary of an event before or after diving into significant details separately.

In the details unveiled in chapter 11, God's reasoning for splitting the people up into different lands with brand-new, different languages is clear. The people had boldly rebelled against God's post-Flood command to "multiply, and fill the earth" (Genesis 9:1). Their explicit goal of building a tower, and with it a city, was to avoid being scattered over the earth (Genesis 11:4).

BIBLE REF.
Genesis 9:1
Genesis 11:4

This event took place nearly 100 years after the Flood (2242 B.C.) and is what Genesis 10:25 is referring to when it says the earth was divided in the days of Peleg.

Connecting the event of the Tower of Babel to the real world:

1. Languages — of the thousands of languages around

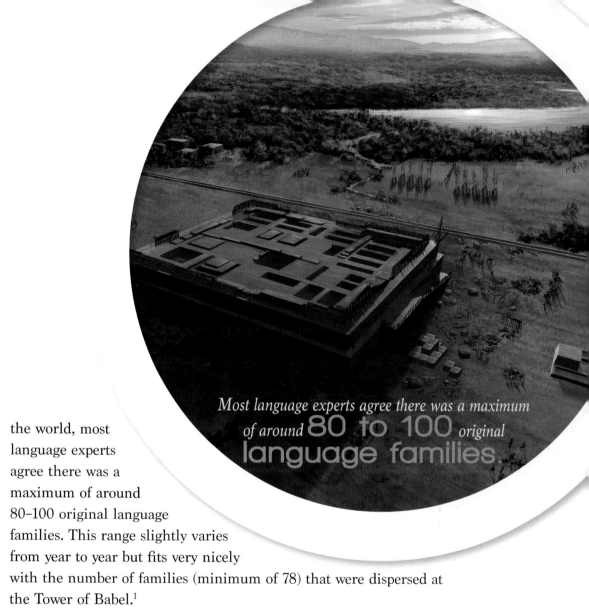

Most language experts agree there was a maximum of around 80 to 100 *original* language families.

the world, most language experts agree there was a maximum of around 80–100 original language families. This range slightly varies from year to year but fits very nicely with the number of families (minimum of 78) that were dispersed at the Tower of Babel.[1]

2. Genealogies — many people groups around the world can trace their family trees back to one of Noah's sons.

3. Ziggurats, mounds and pyramids — these very similar structures are found all over the world. It's almost as if everybody got the same idea from a common source (Tower of Babel was likely a ziggurat) and then spread out and built their own version.[2]

---

1 Compare this to the evolutionary idea that all languages came from one language family of grunting apes! The Christian worldview indeed is in the ballpark.
2 For more on these three subjects, see Bodie Hodge, *The Tower of Babel* (Green Forest, AR: Master Books, 2013).

One race?

So, if all people groups go back to the Tower of Babel, then to Noah's sons, and eventually to Adam and Eve, then how many races are there? One. The human race. All humans are of one blood (Acts 17:26) and have a common ancestor, a real man named Adam — our mutual grandfather.

Why is this so important? The Bible says when Adam and Eve sinned, death entered the world and all of creation was cursed (Genesis 2:3, 17; Romans 8:22). And because all people are their descendants, everyone inherits a sin nature. All people are born in rebellion against their Creator, sinners by nature and choice. This is precisely why Jesus became the Last Adam (Romans 5:12; 1 Corinthians 15:21-22, 45-47). He became one of us, our relative, of our blood, to pay the perfect, infinite price that neither we nor any sacrifice could ever pay.

But if that history in Genesis is not true and there never was a real man named Adam, then where did sin and death come from? Why would Jesus become the Last Adam if there was not a first Adam? You see, both "Adams" are essential to understanding the gospel.

All that being said, how do Christians explain things like different "colors" of skin if everyone is of one race? But are people really different colors? Is a "Caucasian" truly white or an "African-American" truly black? The answer is actually no.

BIBLE REF.
Genesis 2:3, 17
Acts 17:26
Romans 5:12
Romans 8:22
1 Corinthians 15:21-22
1 Corinthians 15:45-47

All people are essentially some shade of brown.

All people are essentially some shade of brown. It's mainly based on a brown pigment called melanin. Some people have more and are a darker shade of brown. Others have less and are a lighter shade of brown. And the majority of the world's population is a middle brown shade. We are all the same color, just different shades.

Some may ask, "But why do different people groups have distinct attributes like different shades?" Answer: the Tower of Babel. It is this event that shows how we got isolated people groups, separated by language and geographical barriers, leading to isolated genetic pools. Within these pools, certain traits became dominant in an area and were passed on from one generation to the next.[1] A common occurrence, genetically speaking.

We are not "red, yellow, black, and white"; we're actually "brown, brown, brown, and brown, different shades of brown."

---

1 For more on this subject, see Ken Ham and Charles Ware, *One Race One Blood* (Green Forest, AR: Master Books, 2010).

An Evolutionary Takeover of Creation

Science vs. the Bible?

How many times have you seen a headline or an advertisement for a television show declaring a battle between "science" and the Bible? It's an extremely popular narrative within our culture with just one major problem — it's dead wrong.

First of all, "science" does not speak, declare, or attack anything. It doesn't make conclusions. Science is a process, a methodology of accumulating certain types of knowledge through experiments that are observable, testable, repeatable, and falsifiable.[1] Scientists, Christian or secular, on the other hand, do make interpretations, statements, and declarations of what they believe to be true.

In reality, there is no conflict between real, observable/repeatable science and the Bible. Most people don't realize that Bible-believing Christians — most of whom believed in a young earth! — started most branches of modern-day science. Johannes Kepler, one of the founders of astronomy, said science was "thinking God's thoughts after Him."

And this makes good sense because without the Bible being true, science would be impossible. It is the Bible that reveals the true Creator God who made the laws of nature and maintains their consistency by the power of His Word (Colossians 1:15–17). If the laws of nature randomly changed (and there is no reason to believe they shouldn't in an evolutionary worldview), then experiments, consistent results, and accumulation of

BIBLE REF.
Colossians 1:15–17

---

1 Science is also probabilistic by nature as well. Any conclusion is not to be seen as absolute but as a probable answer.

In reality, there is no conflict *between* real*, observable/repeatable* science *and the* Bible*.*

knowledge would be impossible. Thus, science would be impossible (it is actually science **because of** the Bible)!

Now comes the crux of the matter. When attempting to figure out what happened in the unseen past, like origins, for example, this can be called "historical science." And it's a different ball game all together from what might be called "observational science." Why? The past is **gone**. It is **not** observable, testable, repeatable, or falsifiable. Without an eyewitness account, the best a person can do is look at the present-day evidence and make a **guess** about the past.

That guess will flow **directly** from a person's assumptions about the past. Those assumptions are rooted in a belief system called a worldview. The question is not the evidence; the question is which worldview do you use to interpret the evidence to understand the past. Do you trust the eyewitness account of the Creator God as revealed in the Bible? Or do you trust the opinions of fallible men who weren't there and don't know even a fraction of all knowledge? Bottom line, the issue is not science vs. the Bible; the battle is man's word being the absolute authority vs. God's Word from a God who is absolute.

What is evolution and where did it come from?

From a big-picture perspective, the evolutionary worldview is the idea that all life on earth has a common ancestor. That, somehow, life came into existence around 3.5 billion years ago and changed over long periods of time, increasing in complexity and diversifying into all the variations of life seen today. To be more specific, some use the phrase "molecules-to-man" evolution or "electron-to-engineer." Or our favorite definition, "from the goo to you through the zoo." But in reality, evolution at its core is an attempt of a pagan culture to explain life without God.

And this attempt to overthrow God as Creator with this false evolutionary view is nothing new. Actually, the idea of evolution is quite ancient.

The Mayan culture, which began around 600 B.C., incorporated a form of evolution into its religion. They believed the rain-god created humans by modifying previous creations: rivers were changed to fish, then to serpents, and finally to humans.[1]

The Greeks were teaching about evolution as early as the 7th century B.C. But it appears they borrowed many of their evolutionary ideas from the Babylonians, Egyptians, and Indians. For example, one ancient Hindu belief in India suggests the universe spontaneously evolved and like a seed it grew and diversified into everything that exists over billions of years.[2]

1 *Encyclopaedia Britannica*, The Werner Co., New York, Vol. 23, p. 467, 1898.
2 From *The Mundaka Upanishad*, Understanding Hinduism, pp. 5–9; keep in mind, though, that

BIBLE REF.
Psalm 119:104
Psalm 119:128
1 John 4:1

Sounds familiar.

From 600–100 B.C., numerous Greek philosophers taught many of today's "modern" ideas about evolution:

Evolution *at its core is an attempt of a pagan culture to explain life* **without God.**

- Anaximander (610–546 B.C.) — humans originally resembled fish[3]

- Democritus (460–370 B.C.) — primitive people grunted and eventually evolved to use words[4]

- Empedocles (493–435 B.C.) — chance caused evolution of matter into man, life came from spontaneous generation, organisms evolved by natural selection.[5]

- Epicurus (341–270 B.C.) — the universe came about by a chance movement of atoms, no god required[6]

On and on the list could go. In the 200 years preceding Darwin's arrival onto the scene, essentially every one of "his ideas" was articulated in quite some detail by other writers and scientists.[7]

It has rightly been said that Darwin did not invent evolution; he just made it popular for a pagan culture desperate for a life without God. Like Solomon said, there is nothing new under the sun.

---

in Hinduism, everything is actually an illusion, including their understanding of origins. This is called the doctrine of Maya.

3 Jonathan Barnes, *Early Greek Philosophy* (London, England: Penguin Books, 1987), p. 72.

4 Paul Cartledge, *Democritus* (London, England: Phoenix, 1998), pp. 20–21.

5 Henry Fairfield Osborn, *From the Greeks to Darwin* (New York: Charles Scribner's Sons, 1929), p. 52.

6 *The Epicurus Reader: Selected Writings and Testimonia*, translated and edited by Brad Inwood and L.P. Gerson, introduction by D.S. Hutchinson (Indianapolis, Indiana: Hackett Publishing Company, 1994).

7 Dr. Jerry Bergman, "Evolutionary Naturalism: An Ancient Idea," Answers in Genesis, August 1, 2001, https://answersingenesis.org/theory-of-evolution/evolutionary-naturalism-an-ancient-idea/.

Origin of life?

This is perhaps one of the most perplexing questions for secular scientists to attempt to answer. How does one explain the origin of life (called *chemical evolution*) if God has been removed from the equation and all that's left are natural processes? The evolutionists often appeal to the "Miller Experiment," but that didn't even come close to making life.

The Miller Experiment was tried in hopes of going against the laws of science. You see, there is a scientific law called the *Law of Biogenesis*. If something has been deemed a "scientific law," that means nothing has ever been observed to the contrary. And the *Law of Biogenesis* states that life only comes from life. That's all that has ever been observed. No one has ever seen a rock give birth to anything!

There is yet another unsurmountable problem for the evolutionist. Life is full of unfathomable amounts of information called DNA. The *Second Law of Information* declares that information always originates from a mind. Now once the information has been obtained, it is possible to make copies of it, but the source of the initial information is always a mind. Yet the secularist has to believe that natural processes produced all this information from inanimate matter (e.g., all the DNA that exists!). This is in direct opposition to observed laws of science.

Thus, the evolutionist is left grasping at straws. Many secular scientists today have turned to the idea of "panspermia" or

BIBLE REF.
Isaiah 45:18

The Law of Biogenesis states that life *only* comes from life.

"directed panspermia." This is the speculation that life on earth originated from an alien source. They propose that maybe simple alien life was transported to earth by something like a meteorite or intelligent aliens came to earth and purposely seeded life on earth and it evolved from there.

We can simply ask how did this *other supposed life* arise in the universe? Evolutionists are just pushing the same problem elsewhere. These sorts of speculations are what one is left with when God has been banned and nature has been deemed god.

On the flipside, these laws are expected within the biblical worldview. The Bible reveals the Creator God is not bound by laws of nature, as He is the One who upholds them. He made nature, the laws of nature, and all life by the power of His Word. Life is a supernatural creation of the God of life, a truth confirmed by real science and the laws of science.

Animal variations– natural selection– mutations

"Look at all the variations of dogs around the world! And they are constantly changing! That proves evolution, right?!" Wrong.

Of course, animals change; no informed, reasonable person argues they don't. Dogs make different dogs, cats make different cats, elephants make different elephants, etc. This is exactly what the Bible teaches when it says God made animals according to their kinds and then told them to reproduce. And since the fall of Genesis 3, natural selection and mutations are the primary engine that drives the change observed today.

But can natural selection and mutations lead to "molecules-to-man" evolution? Changing a fish into a dog, a dinosaur into a bird, or an ape into a man? In order for them to make this kind of change they **must** *add* brand-new, specified, complicated genetic information. Do they? Here's a quick look at natural selection [which was originally developed by a Christian, by the way, years before Darwin] and mutations.

Natural Selection is probably best known by the phrase, "survival of the fittest." It is a name given to a process when certain individuals with certain traits survive better in a given environment and pass on those traits to the next generation. For example, let's say a group of dogs with genetic information for long, medium, and short fur moves to a cold environment. After a while, the dogs with medium and short fur will either

BIBLE REF.
Genesis 30

Mutations **rearrange, destroy**, *or* **delete** *existing genetic information, but based on observations, they* **do not add** *new genetic information required for evolutionary changes.*

freeze and die or move away. Thus, only the dogs with the genetic information for long fur will be left in that environment. They will then pass that trait on to their offspring, and eventually all the dogs in that cold environment will have long fur. That's natural selection. Notice, dogs are still dogs, and the end result of the process is **less** genetic information since they lost the information for short fur.

- Mutations are mistakes within the genome that occur when genetic information is damaged or changed (e.g., six fingers on a person or cancer). Although many are classed as neutral (don't change proteins much), these random and rare mutations are extremely harmful and very often lethal. Mutations are neutral at best but usually detrimental—this is why people (including evolutionists) do not go stand in front of an X-ray machine. It causes bad mutations quickly. Bottom line, mutations rearrange, destroy, or delete existing genetic information, but based on observations, they do not add new genetic information required for evolutionary changes.

All that is ever **observed** through natural selection and mutations is a **mixing** or **loss** of **already**-existing genetic information. Regardless of how much time you give them, these processes cannot lead to "goo-to-you" evolution because no matter how you slice it, losing is not gaining.

Missing links?

Yet another big problem for "molecules-to-man" evolution is that it has never been observed. This is actually quite devastating since observations are vital for something to be "scientific"! No one has ever witnessed one "kind" of animal in the process of changing into a totally different "kind." For example, no one has ever seen a "tyrannosaurus-turkey"— that is, an alleged T-rex changing into a turkey.

Now an evolutionist would likely retort, "Evolution happens too slowly; that's why we can't see it happening today." We would argue that some sort of active transitioning should be visible even today, but even so, there should be an abundance of evidence for this change in the fossil record. Even Charles Darwin, though he couldn't find the transitions in his day, suggested they would soon be found throughout the fossil record to vindicate him. Unfortunately for the evolutionist, the missing links are still missing.

If evolution were true, there should be billions, probably trillions, of fossilized, transitional, intermediate forms of one kind of animal changing into another over the supposed millions of years. They are just not there. There are only a handful of disputed intermediates that the evolutionists are willing to fight over, and those are easily debunked with an honest look at the evidence. The bigger point is the multiplied billions are missing in action.

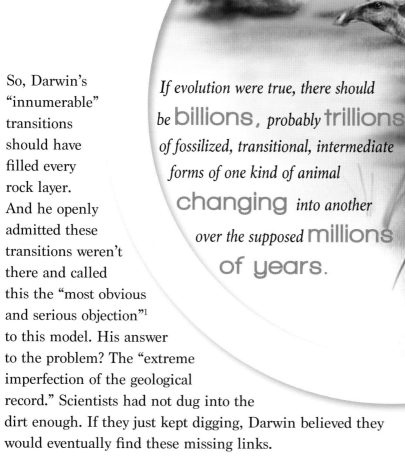

So, Darwin's "innumerable" transitions should have filled every rock layer. And he openly admitted these transitions weren't there and called this the "most obvious and serious objection"[1] to this model. His answer to the problem? The "extreme imperfection of the geological record." Scientists had not dug into the dirt enough. If they just kept digging, Darwin believed they would eventually find these missing links.

If evolution were true, there should be billions, *probably* trillions *of fossilized, transitional, intermediate forms of one kind of animal* changing *into another over the supposed* millions of years.

Well, it's now over 150 years past Darwin, and there are approximately 100 million fossils in museums around the world. And a very honest evolutionist admitted, "knowledge of the fossil record has been greatly expanded. . . . Ironically we have even **fewer** examples of evolutionary transitions than we had in Darwin's time."[2] How many did Darwin actually have? Zero. Today we have less than that . . . too bad for that *tyrannosaurus-turkey*!

1 Charles Darwin, *Origin of the Species*, 6th edition (1956), pp. 292-293.
2 David Raup, "Conflicts Between Darwin and Paleontology," *Chicago Field Museum Bulletin* 50 (January 1979): 22–29.

What about ape-men?

So, if the missing links are missing, then what about all the "ape-men" that secular scientists keep parading as evidence of evolution? When they find a lemur, ape, or human fossil, news headlines abound with "missing link found!"

Then as time unfolds, we come to find out that it is not a missing link but merely a lemur, ape, or a human. So, they keep looking. This is why the secularists today are so desperate to find anything that they can hail as a missing link.

There are three ways people attempt to make missing links:

- First, they take an ape and dress it up to look like a person (e.g., inserting human eyes, human feet, human hands, human jaws, etc.).

- Second, they take a human and try to dress it up like an ape (inserting ape eyes, ape feet, ape hands, ape jaws, etc.).

- Third, people try to make a missing link by taking bones of a human and bones of an ape and trying to build a missing link. But are they real creatures? Nope.

Although there are no evolutionary missing links, we do have common ancestors — Noah, Adam, Eve, and others! But these are not transitions between an ape-like creature and you. Instead, we are all variations of the human kind, all of whom are made in the image of the Creator God.

BIBLE REF.
Genesis 1:26–27
Acts 17:26

We are all variations of the human kind, *all of whom are* made in the image of the Creator God.

Same evidence: two different interpretations

Once again, secular and biblical scientists alike have the same present-day evidence, the same animals, fossils, mutations, natural processes, scientific laws, and methods. And as stated before, this is ultimately a battle of **world-views** that lead to very different interpretations. A battle of the only two fundamental religions: man's word vs. God's Word.

Those who elevate man's word over God's basically assume the way things operate and change in the present is the way they have always done so in the unseen past. **Before** even looking at the evidence, they **assume** the Bible is false and **believe** only present-day, natural processes may be used to explain origins.

Now if the evolutionist were consistent, this approach to the evidence presents some serious difficulties. In accordance with the way things happen now: something never comes from nothing, life never comes from non-life, information never comes from inanimate matter, and natural selection and mutations mix or lose genetic information. All of these present-day, observed realities make evolution impossible. But they are not enough to shake the **blind faith** of the secularist who declares, "nature found a way."

But all of these things are perfectly consistent within a biblical worldview. Of course, natural processes cannot bring time, space, matter, life, and information into existence. That

BIBLE REF.
Psalm 147:5
1 Corinthians 1:20

The biblical interpretation *of the evidence is consistent with* all of reality *and* observational science.

requires the divine act of a God outside of the natural world, the God who has revealed Himself and our origins in His Word. Why is there death and thus natural selection in this world? Because man sinned and death came as consequence. Why do things run down and mutations accumulate? Because of the curse that affected everything when man fell into sin.

The biblical interpretation of the evidence is consistent with all of reality and observational science. In contrast, the evolutionary interpretation is fervently adhered to by its believers in spite of all the laws of science it breaks.

A Christ-Redeemed Creation

What is the gospel?

You might have heard that the word "gospel" means "good news." And indeed it does. But in order to understand the "good news," one must first understand the bad news.

The bad news begins in Genesis. When Adam, the first man, sinned, death and the curse entered this world as a consequence. Since we're all descendants of Adam, we all inherited his legacy of sin and death. Every one of us is a sinner by nature and by choice, in glad rebellion against our Creator. Romans 3:23 puts it like this: "all have sinned and fall short of the glory of God."

You might object and say, "I'm a pretty good person." But good according to whom? God's standard for goodness, and thus His requirement to get into His Heaven, is absolute perfection, never breaking any of His laws your entire life, not even once. Just a quick look at the Ten Commandments reveals our extreme imperfection. It is safe to say anyone who is reading this has been involved in sin against God, whether they realize it or not. Many have surely told numerous lies, stolen something (physical or something immaterial, like reputation or innocence), disrespected parents (to their face or behind their back), worshipped an idol (God wasn't first in your life), coveted something, taken God's name in vain, committed sexual activity outside of marriage, etc. And that's not even all the Ten Commandments!

On top of this, God requires that all of our thoughts and

BIBLE REF.
Romans 3:23
1 John 4:7–8
Psalm 9:8
Psalm 11:7
Rev. 20:11-15

motives be holy and perfect our whole lives. Never a selfish, lustful, hateful, prideful thought, or motive. The list could go on, but that's enough to make any honest person say, "Besides Jesus, no one could do this!" And that's the point — we all fall short. That's the bad news.

Some would then argue, "But God is loving. He wouldn't send me to hell." God is loving; He is the source of all love (1 John 4:7-8). And in His perfect love, He is a perfect and just judge (Psalm 9:8, 11:7, 96:13, Romans 2:16, Revelation 20:11-15). And any just judge will not allow the guilty to go free. And we are all guilty. The bad news just got worst.

But that's why the "good news" is so good! In His love for us, God became flesh, lived a perfect life, died on the cross for our sins as a perfect sacrifice, paid the infinite price we could never pay by taking the wrath of God we deserve, and rose again, defeating death once and for all (1 John 4:9-10; Romans 5:14-19)! The Bible says that while we were still sinners Christ died for us (Romans 5:8) and that anyone who would repent of (turn away from) their sins, confess Jesus as Lord (God, King), and believe that God raised Him from the dead will be saved (John 3:16; Romans 10:9)!

Salvation cannot be earned by "works"; it is the **free gift** of God to all who believe (Ephesians 2:8-9). And that truly is good news!

Using creation in evangelism

As stated from the outset of this book, Answers in Genesis is a biblical-authority ministry, defending God's Word where it's being attacked today. But we dare not stop there. The ultimate motivation for giving a defense is so we can then go on to share the gospel boldly and effectively in secular culture.

Unfortunately, many today don't believe the gospel because they don't believe the book from which the gospel comes. They have fallen prey to the Genesis 3 attack of our day and believed the lie that the history of the Bible is wrong. They have swallowed the enemy's claims that archeology, astronomy, geology, biology, evolution, and millions of years have disproved the Bible. So, the logical conclusion for them is if the Bible's history is false, why trust what it says about salvation? And of course they're right. If the Bible begins with a lie that is reiterated through the rest of the book, why believe anything it says?

So, we give answers, equipping ourselves and the coming generations to answer the skeptical questions of this age by standing on the authority of God's Word, and training ourselves to start at the beginning and use biblical history, a biblical worldview, to understand the past, present, and future. When we do that, the gospel comes alive, and it becomes clear that real, observable science confirms the Bible again and again, that only the biblical worldview makes sense of all of reality.

BIBLE REF.
Romans 1:16

It is the gospel alone that is **the power of God** *unto salvation.*

This demonstrates to a watching world that you can believe the Bible from beginning to end. You can trust what it says about history, and you can trust what it says about salvation. Why? Because it is the very Word of God.

In giving these answers, we demolish the excuses the unbeliever has set up to reject the gospel — but we do this in love because we, too, were "in their same shoes" in the past. We want to humbly unveil the reality of their rebellious heart and desperate need of a Savior. Then we give the gospel. Because it is the gospel alone that is the power of God unto salvation (Romans 1:16)!

Ultimately, we give answers to get to **The Answer**, Jesus Christ.

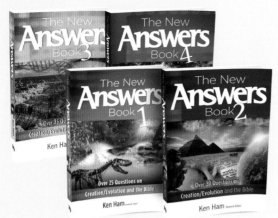
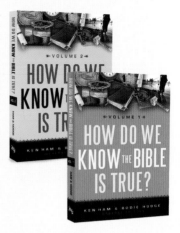

More Answers

Find additional information on the topics in this book with *The New Answers Book* series and the *How Do We Know the Bible is True* series, both from Master Books: